YOUR KNOWLEDGE HAS VALUE

Moritz Deutschmann

The Second World War as the second foundation of the Soviet Union

GRIN Verlag

Bibliografische Information der Deutschen Nationalbibliothek:

Die Deutsche Bibliothek verzeichnet diese Publikation in der Deutschen National-
bibliografie; detaillierte bibliografische Daten sind im Internet über http://dnb.d-
nb.de/ abrufbar.

Imprint:

Copyright © 2007 GRIN Verlag GmbH
Druck und Bindung: Books on Demand GmbH, Norderstedt Germany
ISBN: 978-3-640-31558-1

This book at GRIN:

http://www.grin.com/en/e-book/77953/the-second-world-war-as-the-second-foun-
dation-of-the-soviet-union

University of California, Berkeley
Department of History
Spring 2007
History 280: War and Memory

Moritz Deutschmann

The Second World War as the "Second Foundation" of the Soviet Union

Contents

1 Introduction

"No one will forget, and nothing will be forgotten". This classical Soviet slogan about the Second World War conveys many of the meanings of the Soviet War memory. First, it simply describes a reality: no country which has lost so many of its citizens in the War as the Soviet Union can forget, and still today, almost every family in Russia, the Ukraine, Belarus and many of the other states of the former Soviet Union remembers parents and grandparents who were killed during the War. For a whole generation, the War was the formative experience of a lifetime, an unforgettable memory indeed, and although the number of veterans is diminishing, there still exist enough to tell their stories.

However, the saying also has political significance, as it crowns many of the countless War monuments which can be found everywhere in the former Soviet Union today. They were meant to set the memory of the Soviet victory in stone and to translate the lessons of the wartime experience to future generations. In order to achieve this, the state did not rely on the private memory of its citizens, but, especially since the mid-1960s, organized an all-encompassing cult to commemorate the victory and to make it, together with the October Revolution, the second defining historical event for Soviet socialism.

At the same time, "no one will forget, and nothing will be forgotten" was also a typical Soviet slogan: what it said was quite different from reality. Many aspects of the War were indeed forgotten or, at least, the state tried to make its citizens forget them. There were no monuments for the Soviet invasion of Poland, the deportation of millions of people within the Soviet Union, or the soldiers who were lucky enough to survive German concentration camps, only to be treated as traitors and sometimes even ending up in the GULAG after their return to the Soviet Union.

But Perestroika and Glasnost' finally added an ironic twist to this story of Soviet forgetting and remembering, because at the end of the 80s, the promise not to forget turned against the Soviet system itself. The opening of the archives has revealed most of the hitherto concealed aspects of the War. Newspapers were full of articles questioning the official narrative of the Soviet victory, thus undermining the political system as a whole.

These intended and unintended meanings of "no one will forget and nothing will be forgotten" show how intimately linked post-war Soviet history and the memory of the Second World War are. In fact, there are few aspects of Soviet society after 1945 that do not relate, in one way or the other, to the War: from new relations between the state and its citizens, between countryside and city to generational structure and the nationality conflicts within the

Soviet empire. In this paper, I would like to sketch out some of these relations and ask how collective memory of the War was connected to social change in postwar Soviet society.

2 The Initial Silence

A Soviet soldier who returned to his home country after 1945 held very conflicting feelings: on the one hand, the War had brought the death of many loved ones, unimaginable destruction, and years of extreme material scarcity which even overshadowed the harsh experiences of the 1930s.[1] There had been few times in Russian history where human lives seemed to be of so little value. However, the survivors were often also filled with a tremendous pride for their achievements-- a feeling that they were the true saviors of the motherland. In Vyacheslav Kondratev's post-war novel, the hero remembers: "In the War we were the most necessary of the necessary."[2] There was a wide-spread feeling that this was truly a people's war, not the achievement of Stalin alone. At the same time, the War brought limited relaxation to many repressive policies, for example in the regime's relation to the Orthodox Church. For some, the disastrous year 1941 thus appeared as a spontaneous de-Stalinization and was even greeted as a period of relative freedom.[3]

A certain distance to the regime was especially common among the soldiers who had left their home country for the first time and experienced how much richer even the devastated Poland was than the Soviet Union. After returning to the Soviet Union, many soldiers expected to be rewarded for their sacrifices and hoped for political relaxation and fast economic recovery. A network of veterans emerged, i.e. in the so-called "Blue Danubes" pubs, where veterans talked openly about their War experience and cultivated the spirit of the front experience.[4]

However, these feelings did not translate into any serious political threat for the regime. The soldiers of 1945 did not become the new Dekabrists, as the wide-spread comparison between the "Great Patriotic War" and the Napoleonic Wars would have suggested. All political aspirations were overshadowed by the private concerns of the soldiers who had tremendous difficulties returning to civil life, restoring relations with their often decimated

---

[1] For an overview of the post-war years compare: Fitzpatrick, Sheila: *Postwar Soviet Society. The Return to Normalcy 1945-1953*, in: Susan Linz (ed.), *The Impact of World War II on the Soviet Union*, pp. 129-156. Zubkova, Elena: *Obshchestvo i Reformy 1945-1964*, Moskva 1993.

[2] Zubkova, *Obshchestvo i reformy*, pp. 21.

[3] Tumarkin, Nina: *The Living and the Dead. The Rise and Fall of the Cult of World War II in Russia*, New York 1994, pp. 65. This is especially true for the intellectuals, comp. Bonwetsch, Bernd: *War as a ``Breathing Space". Intellectuals and the "Great Patriotic War"*, in: Robert Thurston / Bernd Bonwetsch (eds.), *The People's War. Responses to World War II in the Soviet Union*, Urbana 2000, pp. 137-154.

[4] Comp. Zubkova, *Obshchestvo i reformy*, pp. 28.

families, and finding work and housing. The last thing they were interested in was another period of violence and political instability.[5] In her study of post-war popular literature, Vera Dunham shows how the strive for a better material life replaced the original ascetic fervor of the 1920s and 30s and created an almost bourgeois pleasure for the good life.[6] The victory gave survivors pride and self-esteem, but only very few questioned Stalin's leadership or the socialist system in general which had, in many people's eyes, proven its superiority over capitalism in the victory.[7]

Although Stalin's government was not directly in danger, Stalin was anxious to renew his grip on society. The system of compulsory labor from the War years was not abolished, but used to speed up the reconstruction. Many of the soldiers were directly integrated into a system of militarized labor.[8] After the immediate post-war years, the Zhdanovshina brought a repression in the cultural realm; and although the mass terror of the thirties did not reappear, events like the Leningrad Affair or the so-called "Doctors' Plot", which was directed against the Jewish population, were clear reminders of the arbitrary nature of Stalin's leadership.

This repression was accompanied by a remarkable silence about the War. Whereas in Western Europe and the US, thousands of memoirs and books were already published in the mid 1950s, there was only a very small number of Soviet books and films on the War at that time; the publication of private memoirs was severely restricted.[9] After the anniversary of the German capitulation had been celebrated as a national, work-free holiday for the first time in 1946, by 1947 it was downgraded to one of the Soviet "working holidays".[10] Popular War heroes, most prominently General Zhukov, quickly fell into disgrace or even ended up in prison camps. Whereas in many of the new satellite states, for example in East Germany, the Soviet government was quick to build monuments to remind the population how much they owed the Soviet Union for their liberation from Nazism, this process did not start in the Soviet Union itself until the 1960s.[11] The official number of deaths, 7 million, was deliberately undercounted[12] and social services for war veterans were almost nonexistent. Perhaps the most brutal sign that the War was literally removed from public memory was the sudden disappearance of many disabled veterans from the streets of Moscow and Leningrad in

---

[5]   Ibid., pp. 26.
[6]   Dunham, Vera: *In Stalin's Times. Middle-class Values in Soviet Fiction*, Cambridge 1976.
[7]   Zubkova, *Obshchestvo i reformy*, pp. 26.
[8]   Comp. Filtzner, Donald: *Soviet Workers and Late Stalinism*, Cambridge 2002.
[9]   Ibid., pp. 171.
[10]   Bonwetsch, Bernd: *Der 'Große Vaterländische Krieg'. Vom öffentlichen Schweigen unter Stalin zum Heldenkult unter Brezhnev*, in: Babette Quinkert (ed.), *'Wir sind die Herren dieses Landes'. Ursachen, Verlauf und Folgen des deutschen Überfalls auf die Sowjetunion*, Hamburg 2002, pp. 166-187.
[11]   Ibid, pp. 172. Compare also Tumarkin, *The Living and the Dead*, pp. 101.
[12]   Ibid., pp. 173.

1947. They disturbed the image of the progressive, young and modern Soviet city, and were deported to special camps on the countryside.[13]

The potential of war memory to challenge Stalin's leadership became apparent in some of the hidden power struggles which took place in the post-war years. In Leningrad, the local party elite emphasized its own, independent role in the blockade of the city and used the War memory to increase its reputation in Moscow. Already in 1943, a local commission started to collect material to document the history of the blockade and a museum was opened in 1944.[14] This strategy was first successful, as the ascent of the Leningrad party leader Andrei Zhdanov showed, who gave post-war culture politics its name.[15] However, the Leningrad Affair of 1949, parts of which are still mysterious today, drastically reduced the influence of the Leningrad party committee which had become too powerful in Stalin's eyes. Remarkably, this change in the power structure was accompanied by an almost complete silencing of the commemoration of the blockade; even in 1954, ten years after the end of the blockade, nobody dared to hold an official celebration.[16] Only in 1956, Khrushchev gave a signal in one of his speeches that it was once again legitimate to commemorate the blockade in public, but this time as an achievement of the Soviet people in general. Ironically, one of the motives for Khrushchev's move was probably that he relied on the support of the Leningrad party officials, Malenkov and Beria, in his power struggle.[17]

3   The Expected Armaggedon

It seems that the War memory was, starting from the very end of the War, a highly ambivalent and delicate matter in the relations between the state and its people. The War could be taken as a victory for socialism, an affirmation of the existing social order, but it also offered a huge potential for opponents of the regime. Probably the most thorough study of this complex relationship between power and memory in the post-war years is Amir Weiner's book "Making Sense of War".

Weiner sees the War and its memory in the context of the larger Communist project to create an aesthetically ordered, harmonic Soviet society.[18] This transformation required violence on an unprecedented scale, because constantly new groups of external and internal

---

[13]   Tumarkin, *The Living and the Dead*, pp. 98. Compare also: Merridale, Catherine: *Ivan's War. Life and Death in the Red Army 1939-1945*, New York 2006, pp. 267.
[14]   Ganzenmüller, Jörg: *Das belagerte Leningrad 1941-1944. Die Stadt in den Strategien von Angreifern und Verteidigern*, Paderborn 2005, pp. 327 pass.
[15]   Ibid, pp. 325 pass.
[16]   Ibid, pp. 342.
[17]   Ibid., pp. 343.
[18]   Ibid., pp. 21.

enemies had to be fought, from the remnants of Tsarism and its European allies during the Civil War to the peasants, who resisted collectivization at the beginning of the 1930s, and finally the alleged enemies within the party itself in the second half of the 1930s. The convinced Stalinists of the 30s, therefore, perceived the War against Nazi Germany not as an accident which could have been avoided by means of a different foreign policy, but as an expected Armaggedon, the ultimate struggle between Communism and its ubiquitous enemies. Like in the 1920s and 30s already, external and internal enemies were seen as linked; thus, the fight against the enemy outside required political purification among the own population, above all in the party itself.[19]

Weiner uses the Vinnytsa region in central Ukraine to examine massive purges within the party in the post-war years under which whole population groups came under scrutiny. The extent to which the party renewed itself as a result of war losses and post-war purges is visible in the membership figures: in 1947, less than 25% of the party members had joined the party before the War.[20] The War intensified the tendency already evident in the late 1930s: enemy groups were no longer believed to be reformable and redeemable; the ideological primacy of "nurture" over "nature" was increasingly challenged.[21] Those party members who had lived under German occupation during the War had to prove that they had fought heroically.[22] But often they were globally punished as collaborators, in many cases together with their families.[23] The purges were also a weapon in other social conflicts, for example between the army veterans, whose war effort confirmed the importance of bureaucratic organization, and the veterans of the partisan movement, whose initiative and independent spirit challenged the narrative of Stalin and the party as the main contributor to victory.[24]

The most important struggle, however, took place between Ukrainian nationalists and Soviet Communists. Weiner shows that the Ukrainian nationalists shared with their Communist enemies a totalitarian ethos of social "purity" and order; an order, however, not along social, but along ethnic lines.[25] The Ukrainian nationalist project excluded the Jewish population, whom it identified with Soviet power.[26] In many cases, Ukrainian nationalists even collaborated in the extermination of the Jews during the War.

---

[19] Weiner, Amir: *Making Sense of War. The Second World War and the Fate of the Bolshevik Revolution*, Princeton 2001, pp. 21 pass.
[20] Ibid., pp. 125.
[21] Ibid., pp. 26.
[22] Ibid., pp. 86.
[23] Ibid., pp. 125.
[24] Ibid., pp. 70.
[25] Ibid., pp. 240 pass.
[26] Ibid., pp. 273.

7

Although from this point of view, the memory of the War excluded many from the Soviet victory, it also provided new possibilities for integration into Soviet society. Most stunning are the changes on the countryside: whereas in the 1930s, the peasants were considered backward, reactionary forces, who were obstacles on the Soviet path to an industrialized, modern society, the War made them into heroes and opened them new social opportunities. Many of the peasants depicted their enlistment in the Red Army as the turning point in their biographies, even when they had been persecuted as Kulaks in the early 1930s.[27] Ukrainian nationalists who used the memory of the resistance to the Soviet collectivization drive in the 1930s to mobilize the peasants could not compete with the integrating force of the Soviet War experience. In the end, the Soviet regime, not the nationalists, established itself as the creator of a unified Ukrainian nation and even encouraged a sense of Ukrainian nationhood within a larger Soviet patriotism.[28]

The War was a means of social ascent and produced a remarkable social group, a whole generation of heroes, which would occupy many leadership positions in the Soviet Union until 1991. The prominent dissident Ludmilla Alexeyeva describes in her memoirs how she encountered these ambitious "frontoviki" while studying at Moscow University in the 1950s. Many of them were uneducated peasant boys who had entered the Komsomol or the party during the War: "The war had given them a taste of power and now they were determined to stay in the city for the rest of their lives. Most of them visualized the same career ladder: a degree in the history of the USSR or the history of the Communist party, then a position somewhere in the party apparatus".[29]

4   The Memory Cult

The Thaw ended the relative silence about the War which had prevailed under Stalin. A number of films and novels about the War appeared which generally showed the suffering of the War more realistically than under Stalin.[30] The number of dead was corrected to 20 million, still an underestimate, but at least closer to the truth. One of the central points in Khrushchev's critique of Stalin's cult of personality was Stalin's role during the War and his mistakes in military strategy. In general, Khrushchev gave much more credit to the war efforts of the population in general. However, even during the Thaw, there were still many things

---

[27]   Ibid., pp. 323.
[28]   Ibid., pp. 336.
[29]   Alexeyeva, Ludmilla / Goldberg, Paul: *The Thaw Generation. Coming of Age in the Post-Stalin Era*, Boston 1990, pp. 30.
[30]   Tumarkin, *The Living and the Death*, pp. 112.

that could not to be uttered. This becomes obvious in the history of probably the most famous novels about the War, Ivan Grossmann's "Life and Faith" which was not allowed to be published in 1960.[31] The book contained a whole series of provocations, including a comparison by one of the protagonists between Hitler's and Stalin's regimes.[32]

An important reason why the book was not published was the open descriptions of the Holocaust. The particular fate of the Jewish population remained a taboo topic in the Soviet Union after the War; even in cases of obvious mass murders, as in Babi Yar, the official history talked about the murder of "Soviet citizens" or "innocent civilians" without stressing the Jewish identity of the victims. The suffering of the Jews should not overshadow the narrative of the suffering of the Soviet people as a whole.[33] On the other hand, the contribution of Jewish soldiers to the victory was systematically downplayed: rumors about the absence of Jews at the front were wide-spread; in fact, many Jews had kept their identity secret, because they feared the anti-Semitism among the Soviet soldiers as well as the consequences if they were taken prisoners by the enemy.[34] The Jews did not appear as a specific group of victims, and were at the same time excluded from the Soviet pantheon of heroes.

The popularization of the War under Khrushchev laid the foundation for the emergence of a true cult of memory of the War which emerged in the mid-1960s under Brezhnev: the 9th of May became a holiday again; war literature was published in huge numbers: between 1965 and 1988, over 20,000 books on the War with a total circulation of one billion were published.[35] Almost all leading figures in the military who had fought in the War published their memoirs, which were censored by a special commission set up in the ministry of defense.[36] From the mid-60s on, a large number of War monuments were built, for example the famous "Rodina Mat'" complex ("Motherland") which commemorated the battle of Stalingrad. The War started to permeate private life: it became custom for couples to stop at the local War monument during their wedding ceremony to take pictures. The local monument was also the place, where 16-year-olds were given their first Soviet passport. The Brezhnev era brought countless improvements for War veterans, for example special lines in shops. The veteran who constantly wore his medals in order to be the first person in line

---

[31]   Ibid., pp. 113.
[32]   Ibid., pp. 114.
[33]   Weiner, *Making Sense of War*, pp. 208.
[34]   Ibid., pp. 221.
[35]   Bonwetsch, *Der 'Große Vaterländische Krieg'*, pp. 176.
[36]   Ibid., pp. 177.

became a common phenomenon in Soviet everyday life, often arousing anger and contempt in the population.[37]

A good impression of how the Brezhnevian narrative of the War was presented in high-school textbooks.[38] Usually, the War appeared as a result of Western imperialism and of the rivalry between Germany, Italy, and Japan on the one hand, and France, Britain and the US on the other.[39] The beginning of the War was in this perspective merely an "armed skirmish of the two imperialist coalitions."[40] In spite of their internal conflicts, the alleged ultimate goal of all sides was the destruction of the Soviet Union.[41] This account of the War connected the feeling of encirclement and universal hostility, which were so typical of Soviet political culture from the 1920s on, to the Cold War experience.

The textbook emphasizes the contribution to the victory the Soviet people made as a whole---Stalin is hardly mentioned in the narrative---apart from that, the names of some of the generals figure prominently in the description of events. The authors also highlight the role of individual, paradigmatic heroes, who sacrificed themselves for their country, but does not include the experience of larger parts of the population.[42] Although the former captives were often treated as traitors in the immediate post-war years, they are also depicted as participants in the struggle against the German occupation.[43] The Jewish victims only appear once, and in a very minor position: "A million and a half Russians, Poles, Czechs, Jews, Frenchmen and Dutchmen were killed at Maidanek by the Fascist butchers."[44] The book concludes on an optimistic note, depicting the War as a victory for socialism and integrating it into a larger picture of the coming of a socialist society: "The conditions had now been created for the transformation of socialism into a world-wide system...Socialism spread beyond the confines of one country and embraced a whole string of nations in Europe and Asia; this led to radical changes in the international situation."[45]

It testifies to the importance of these histories that at the end of the 1970s, school curricula dedicated the same number of lessons to the War as to the October Revolution.[46]

---

[37]   Tumarkin, *The Living and The Dead*, pp. 195. A Russian friend told me how she wanted to buy some cheese in a supermarket in the Soviet Union in the 1980s, only to learn that this cheese was "for veterans only".
[38]   Lyons, Graham (ed.): *The Russian Version of the Second World War. The History of the War as Taught to Soviet Schoolchildren*, London 1976.
[39]   Ibid., pp. 1.
[40]   Ibid., pp. 10.
[41]   Ibid., pp. 2.
[42]   Compare for example the description of Ilya Kaplunov, a Komsomol member, who allegedly destroyed nine German tanks before he was killed. Ibid., pp. 52
[43]   Ibid., pp. 75.
[44]   Ibid., pp. 71.
[45]   Ibid., pp. 87.
[46]   Bonwetsch, *Der 'Große Vaterländische Krieg'*, pp.178.

Even today, the influence of the Brezhnevian narrative is visible, for example in the yearly contest for school children organized by the foundation MEMORIAL, in which high school students explore the history of their communities and families. Alongside the more personal memories, in the children's works the canonical slogans for the War from the Brezhnev era still appear, such as "Victory Day - that's joy with tears in the eyes" or "Nobody forgets, and nothing is forgotten."[47]

5 Heroes and Victims

According to Nina Tumarkin, the cult of the War was a means to replace the fading memory of the October revolution.[48] It served as an integrating myth to tie the youth to the veterans and finally to the regime: "It was a kind of counter-campaign against international youth culture and some of the major forces impelling change in the Western world."[49] Tumarkin's book was written during Perestroika and stresses the distance between the way ordinary people remembered the War and the official memory of the regime. In fact, many Western observers have criticized the way in which the Soviet regime used a deeply tragic experience for its own legitimatization and made victims into heroes. The bombastic celebrations of the victory seemed to overshadow the countless personal losses suffered during the War. Jörg Ganzenmüller's study of the blockade of Leningrad impressively shows how this emphasis on victory has hidden much of the reality and suffering of the War. Neither the German side who tried to depict the Wehrmacht as a normal army, ignoring its crucial role in the Vernichtungskrieg, nor the Soviet side, who celebrated the city's heroic resistance, made clear that the goal of the blockade was not the capture of the city, but the starvation of the population. That the blockade was not a heroic military struggle, but in fact an attempted genocide remained unspoken.[50]

But the neglect of human suffering and its subordination to the heroic epic of the "Great Patriotic War" has also inspired different interpretations, as Catherine Merridale's book about death and memory in 20th century Russia shows. Merridale, who has conducted a large number of interviews with survivors of the War, does not consider the concept of individual traumatization, which has been dominant in the Western discourse on war victims, as an adequate way to understand the Soviet experience. She recognized that many of the survivors

[47]   Irina Shcherbakova: *Nad kartoi pamyati*, in: Mikhail Gabovich (ed.), *Pamyat' o voyne 60 let spustya Rossiya Germaniya Evropa*, Moskva 2005, pp. 195-210 (pp. 196).
[48]   Tumarkin, *The Living and the Dead*, pp. 101.
[49]   Ibid., pp. 133.
[50]   Ganzenmüller, *Das belagerte Leningrad*, pp. 368.

still use the Soviet terminology to describe their experiences and avoid depicting themselves as victims; pride rather than self-pity is still their common reaction, many of them think of themselves as members of the "strongest and most valued collective in history".[51] Often, the survivors would point to the necessities of everyday life which made it impossible for them to mourn for a longer time: "Of course it was terrible. But we had to rebuild our town. We were carrying everything ourselves, there was no other way. We had defeated the fascists, and now we were building socialism, right there in Kiew."[52] Hard work and belief in the common goal of a socialist society rather than individual mourning as traumatized victims appear as the most common reaction to the War experience. In Merridale's view, the picture of a huge gulf between the state-drive, propaganda cult around the War and the authentic experience of the population is too simple, because it does not recognize the degree to which the survivors themselves used the picture of the heroic victory to deal with their horrifying experiences.

Other authors emphasize that the commemoration of the tragic aspects of the War was not simply missing, but often took different forms than in the West. Whereas historical science in the Soviet Union remained largely confined to the official interpretation of the War, literature played a key role in depicting more private and individual memories of the War. Anna Krylova shows how literature functioned as a form of a quasi-psychotherapy in the immediate post-war years, whereas the state did not care about the traumatization of many War veterans.[53]

6 No More Blank Spots: the End of the Soviet Union

Gorbachev's policies of glasnost' and perestroika in the 1980s encouraged a much more open approach to the past. The overwhelming desire to finally express and learn the truth was in fact one of the crucial aspects of the political reforms, as Gorbachev made clear during his speech in the commemoration of the 70th anniversary of the Bolshevik Revolution, when he called for the erasure of so-called "blank spots" in Soviet history.[54] There was enormous public interest in history; this is illustrated in the exchange of letters between the historian Samsonov, who published a plethora of historical articles in different newspapers during Perestroika, and his readers from different parts of the Soviet Union.[55] Many of the letters (and also Samsonov's own remarks) refer to the critique of Stalinism which had evolved

[51]   Merridale, Catherine: *Night of Stone. Death and Memory in 20th Century Russia*, London 2001, pp.314.
[52]   Ibid., pp. 328.
[53]   Krylova, Anna: *'Healer of Wounded Souls'. The Crisis of Private Life in Soviet Literature*, in: Journal of Modern History 73(2001), 307-331.
[54]   Tumarkin, *The Living and the Dead*, pp. 164.
[55]   Samsonov, A.M.: *Znat' i pomnit'. Dialog istorika s chitatelem*, Moskva 1988.

during the thaw period. Again and again, the "cult of personality" is attacked and Stalin's role in the War is questioned. For example, one of the veterans remarks that the formulation which appeared in many official condolence letters that a soldier had died with the words "for the fatherland, for Stalin" was wrong.[56]

But even more important was the influence that the new view on the War had on relations between the different nationalities within the Soviet Union. The publication of the secret protocol of the Hitler-Stalin pact supported the claims of the independence movements in the Baltic states.[57] In foreign policy, Glasnost' brought the first public admission of a Soviet regime about the massacre of Polish officers in Katyn in 1940.[58] The 45th anniversary of the victory made these changes visible, as Gorbachev's speech differed very much from those of previous anniversaries: for the first time, the price of the victory and its tragic aspects were officially enunciated.[59]

However, although Perestroika challenged the canonical Soviet narrative of the War in many ways and toppled the Leninist foundations of the Soviet state, the moral legacy of the War remained unchanged. In the intellectually confusing atmosphere of the early 1990s, there were radical revisionist attempts to rehabilitate Vlasov and his army, but this view remained an exception. Today, the War against Germany is the only war in the 20th century that a majority of the Russian population considers to be a just war.[60] Over the last few years, the tendency to emphasize the positive nature of the War has even increased. Whereas practically every other event in Soviet history has come under scrutiny, this victory stands out as the single most positive achievement of more than 70 years of socialism.[61] Thus, the legacy of the War overshadows the October Revolution and remains one of the orientation points of Russian historical memory in the 20th century.

7   War Memory and Post-War Soviet Society

It is amazing that in spite of the "memory boom" in historical sciences in the last years, little has been written about Soviet War memory. Much of the research so far has been occupied with a critique of the bombastic memory cult imposed by the regime. The Cold War as well as personal contact to dissidents and Soviet historians during Perestroika are the

---

[56]   Ibid., pp. 24.
[57]   Tumarkin, *The Living and the Dead*, pp. 175.
[58]   Ibid., pp. 181.
[59]   Ibid., pp. 197.
[60]   Lev Gudkov: *"Pamyat'" o voyne i massovaya identichnost' rossiyan*, in: Mikhail Gabovich (ed.), *Pamyat' o voyne 60 let spustya Rossiya Germaniya Evropa*, 2005, pp. 83-104 (pp. 90).
[61]   Ibid.

background to this view, which becomes apparent in Nina Tumarkin's book, so far the only monograph dedicated solely to the history of War memory.

There are only very few studies which see the War in the larger context of the history of the Soviet experiment. Amir Weiner's book shows the way in which the War was integrated into the larger struggle of the Bolsheviki against external and internal enemies, and was at the same time a tremendous means of Sovietization. This perspective which sees the integrating as well as the exclusionary aspects of the War memory and connects them to the distribution of political power in the Soviet system could be a good starting point for further research on the period after the 1950s, which does not appear in Weiner's book.

In this perspective, it would be important to look more closely for the social basis of the War cult and its limited ability to integrate large groups in Soviet society. This would include a more thorough examination of the private memory of Soviet citizens. Some of the more recent research in Stalinism has emphasized how deeply Stalinist ideas became entrenched even in the most personal ideas of its contemporaries.[62] Soviet power relied not only on open repression, but to a large extent also on its ability to shape the subjective views and memories of individuals. Catherine Merridale's book has given some very interesting ideas in this direction, pointing out how the official narrative of the War, despite its countless falsifications, remained the most influential interpretation of the War and helped the survivors to make sense of their own biographies as Soviet citizens.

---

[62] For example Hellbeck, Jochen: *Revolution on My Mind. Writing a Diary under Stalin*, Cambridge 2006.

8 Bibliography

1. Alexeyeva, Ludmilla / Goldberg, Paul: The Thaw Generation. Coming of Age in the Post-Stalin Era, Boston 1990

2. Bonwetsch, Bernd: Der 'Große Vaterländische Krieg'. Vom öffentlichen Schweigen unter Stalin zum Heldenkult unter Brezhnev, in: Babette Quinkert (ed.), 'Wir sind die Herren dieses Landes'. Ursachen, Verlauf und Folgen des deutschen Überfalls auf die Sowjetunion, Hamburg 2002, pp. 166-187.

3. Bonwetsch, Bernd: War as a ``Breathing Space''. Intellectuals and the "Great Patriotic War", in: Robert Thurston / Bernd Bonwetsch (eds.), The People's War. Responses to World War II in the Soviet Union, Urbana 2000, pp. 137-154.

4. Dunham, Vera: In Stalin's Times. Middle-class values in Soviet fiction, Cambridge 1976.

5. Filtzner, Donald: Soviet Workers and Late Stalinism, Cambridge 2002.

6. Fitzpatrick, Sheila: Postwar Soviet Society. The Return to Normalcy 1945-1953, in: Susan Linz (ed.), The Impact of World War II on the Soviet Union, pp. 129-156.

7. Ganzenmüller, Jörg: Das belagerte Leningrad 1941-1944. Die Stadt in den Strategien von Angreifern und Verteidigern, Paderborn 2005, pp. 327 pass.

8. Irina Shcherbakova: Nad kartoi pamyati, in: Mikhail Gabovich (ed.), Pamyat' o voyne 60 let spustya Rossiya Germaniya Evropa, Moskva 2005, pp. 195-210

9. Krylova, Anna: 'Healer of Wounded Souls'. The Crisis of Private Life in Soviet Literature, in: Journal of Modern History 73(2001), 307-331.

10. Lev Gudkov: "Pamyat'" o voyne i massovaya identichnost' rossiyan, in: Mikhail Gabovich (ed.), Pamyat' o voyne 60 let spustya Rossiya Germaniya Evropa, Moskva 2005, pp. 83-104 (pp. 90).

11. Lyons, Graham (ed.): The Russian Version of the Second World War. The History of the War as Taught to Soviet Schoolchildren, London 1976.

12. Merridale, Catherine: Ivan's War. Life and Death in the Red Army 1939-1945, New York 2006.

13. Merridale, Catherine: Night of Stone. Death and Memory in 20th Century Russia, London 2001.

14. Samsonov, A.M.: Znat' i pomnit'. Dialog istorika s chitatelem, Moskva 1988.

15. Tumarkin, Nina: Tumarkin, Nina: The Living and the Dead. The Rise and Fall of the Cult of World War II in Russia, New York 1994

16. Zubkova, Elena: Obshchestvo i reformy 1945-1964, Moskva 1993.